STEPHEN CURRY

HARDWOOD GREATS

PRO BASKETBALL'S BEST PLAYERS

CHRIS PAUL

GIANNIS ANTETOKOUNMPO

JAMES HARDEN

KEVIN DURANT

LEBRON JAMES

PAUL GEORGE

RUSSELL WESTBROOK

STEPHEN CURRY

HARDWOOD GREATS
PRO BASKETBALL'S BEST PLAYERS

STEPHEN CURRY

DONALD PARKER

MASON CREST
PHILADELPHIA
MIAMI

Mason Crest
450 Parkway Drive, Suite D
Broomall, Pennsylvania 19008
(866) MCP-BOOK (toll-free)
www.masoncrest.com

First printing
9 8 7 6 5 4 3 2 1

ISBN (hardback) 978-1-4222-4352-7
ISBN (series) 978-1-4222- 4344-2
ISBN (ebook) 978-1-4222- 7467-5

Cataloging-in-Publication Data on file with the Library of Congress

Developed and Produced by National Highlights Inc.
Editor: Andrew Luke
Interior and cover design: Annalisa Gumbrecht, Studio Gumbrecht
Production: Michelle Luke

QR CODES AND LINKS TO THIRD-PARTY CONTENT

CONTENTS

KEY ICONS TO LOOK FOR:

Words to Understand: These words with their easy-to-understand definitions will increase the reader's understanding of the text while building vocabulary skills.

Sidebars: This boxed material within the main text allows readers to build knowledge, gain insights, explore possibilities, and broaden their perspectives by weaving together additional information to provide realistic and holistic perspectives.

Educational Videos: Readers can view videos by scanning our QR codes, providing them with additional educational content to supplement the text. Examples include news coverage, moments in history, speeches, iconic sports moments, and much more!

Text-Dependent Questions: These questions send the reader back to the text for more careful attention to the evidence presented there.

Research Projects: Readers are pointed toward areas of further inquiry connected to each chapter. Suggestions are provided for projects that encourage deeper research and analysis.

Series Glossary of Key Terms: This back-of-the-book glossary contains terminology used throughout this series. Words found here increase the reader's ability to read and comprehend higher-level books and articles in this field.

 WORDS TO UNDERSTAND

prodigious: Wonderful or marvelous

reigning: Current

singular: Distinguished by superiority; exceptional

CHAPTER 1

GREATEST MOMENTS

STEPHEN CURRY'S NBA CAREER

Stephen Curry developed a lot of his ability to play basketball early in life. He is the son of former NBA (National Basketball Association) player Dell Curry, who was known as a three-point specialist during his 16-year playing career. He is also the brother of Seth, who is a NBA point guard with the Portland Trailblazers. With all of this talent in the Curry family, he was destined to be good at the sport, but it was hard to predict just how great he would become.

Curry has developed into one of the best three-point shooters in the history of the league.

Steph Curry emerged as one of the best in the game after a 2014–2015 season that saw him lead the league in three-point shots made and attempted, free throw percentage, and steals while averaging 23.8 points per game. Curry led his team, the Golden State Warriors, to a 67–15 record and their first NBA Championship in 40 years. Oh, and by the way, he also was named the league's Most Valuable Player (MVP)!

Curry has developed a deadly outside shot from behind the three-point arc and is also good with his hands as a defensive player. His development as an all-around player and team leader has helped the Warriors establish themselves as one of the best teams in the league and has placed Curry on the path to someday being inducted into the NBA Hall of Fame in Springfield, Massachusetts.

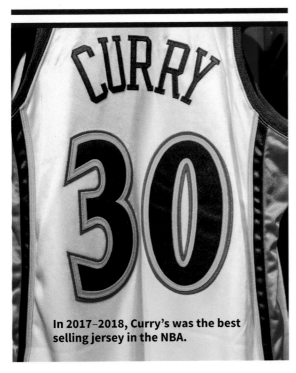
In 2017–2018, Curry's was the best selling jersey in the NBA.

Curry is a three-time NBA champion, two-time league MVP, six-time All-Star, and has been named to the All-NBA team six times in his 10 NBA seasons from 2009 to 2019. There doesn't seem to be any limit to his talent or ability. Curry has accomplished far more in his career than most players could ever hope for and may have a few more chapters to write before his NBA story concludes.

CURRY'S GREATEST CAREER MOMENTS

HERE IS A LIST OF

SOME OF THE CAREER

FIRSTS AND GREATEST

ACHIEVEMENTS DURING

HIS TIME IN THE NBA:

Curry's NBA career has exceeded the expectations of even the most optimistic supporters.

WON FIRST MOST VALUABLE PLAYER AWARD (2014-2015 NBA SEASON)

For Curry, his third year was his breakout year in the NBA. He put up **prodigious** stats in several categories including most three-point shots made (286) and attempted (646), highest free throw percentage (91.4 percent), and most steals (163). His numbers helped lead the Warriors to a 67–15 win-loss record and their first NBA championship since 1975. His efforts that season also led to his being named the league's Most Valuable Player.

Curry's performance during the 2014–2015 NBA season included a 23.8 points-per-game average, a lead in several offensive categories for the season, and a divisional, conference, and league championship on his way to winning his first MVP award for best player.

WON FIRST NBA CHAMPIONSHIP (2014-2015 NBA SEASON)

The 2014–2015 NBA season was a **singular** year for Curry and the Golden State Warriors. Everything fell into place for Curry as he led the team to its most regular season wins—67—in team history (at the time). Coincidentally, just as in 1975 (when the team won 59 games), winning their franchise high number of games led to an appearance in the NBA Finals. There they faced the Eastern Conference Champion Cleveland Cavaliers (led by the return of LeBron James from the Miami Heat). Curry averaged 28.3 points in 21 playoff games (including 26.0 ppg in the six-game NBA Finals) and brought the championship trophy back to Oakland, California.

Curry did all he could to prevent the Warriors from having to face the LeBron James–led Cleveland Cavaliers in a Game 7 by scoring 25 points, dishing out eight assists, and pulling down six rebounds in a 105–97 Game 6 victory for the championship.

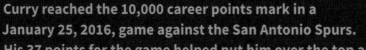

Curry reached the 10,000 career points mark in a
January 25, 2016, game against the San Antonio Spurs.
His 37 points for the game helped put him over the top and in league
with some of the greatest scorers in NBA history.

HARDWOOD GREATS: PRO BASKETBALL'S BEST PLAYERS

WON NBA SCORING TITLE
[2015-2016 NBA SEASON]

Following the 2014–2015 breakout season, what did the league's **reigning** MVP have to do to top his performance? Win the league's scoring title, of course. Curry led the NBA in scoring during the 2015–2016 season, making 805 of 1,598 field goals for a shooting percentage of just over 50 percent. He also went 402 of 886 from the three-point line (45.4 percent shooting) and hit 363 out of 400 free throws for 90.8 percent. He topped off his season of scoring excellence by averaging 30.1 points per game.

Curry makes scoring look too easy! He followed up his 2014–2015 MVP season by winning the award again, averaging 30.1 points and scoring 2,375 points on his way to winning his first NBA scoring title.

WON NBA STEALS TITLE (2014-2015 NBA SEASON)

The year 2015 not only gave Curry his first MVP trophy, but he also won his first NBA Championship with the Warriors and added his first NBA steal title as well. He led the league with 163 ball thefts, averaging two steals a game for the season. His 1,120 career steals puts him among the best in the history of the NBA and ahead of former Golden State great Rick Barry.

Highlights of Curry's ability to get hands on the ball and take it away from the opponent, on his way to winning the 2015 steals title.

BECAME A MEMBER OF THE NBA 50-40-90 CLUB (2015-2016 NBA SEASON)

One of the most difficult clubs for an NBA player to become a member of is the 50–40–90 club. Membership requires a player to have an overall shooting percentage of 50 percent or higher, a three-point shooting percentage of 40 percent or more, and a free throw average of 90 percent or higher. The club, which became a part of the NBA with the introduction of the three-point shot in 1979, has eight members, including Kevin Durant (Oklahoma City Thunder), Mark Price (Cleveland Cavaliers), Reggie Miller (Indiana Pacers), Steve Nash (Phoenix Suns), Dirk Nowitzki (Dallas Mavericks), Jose Calderon (Toronto Raptors), and Larry Bird (Boston Celtics). Nash accomplished the 50–40–90 shooting average on four separate occasions, and Larry Bird in two separate seasons.

Curry joined the 50–40–90 club in 2015–2016, the first scoring leader in league history to do so. He averaged 50.4 percent shooting, 45.4 percent from the three-point line, and 90.8 percent from the three-point line.

NAMED ASSOCIATED PRESS MALE ATHLETE OF THE YEAR (2015)

Curry collected a lot of hardware in 2015. In addition to winning his first NBA Championship as a member of the Golden State Warriors and his first award as the league's Most Valuable Player, he was named the Associated Press (AP) Athlete of the Year for 2015. This award was given to him in recognition of the standout year he had and made him one of only three other NBA players (LeBron James, Michael Jordan, and Larry Bird) to win the award in its 85-year history (as of 2015). He beat out pro golfer Jordan Spieth and triple-crown winner American Pharoah for the honor.

SPORTS › ALERT   AP MALE ATHLETE OF THE YEAR

FOX   f 🖾 @FOXBUSINES

Curry had a wonderful 2015, which ended with his being named AP Male Athlete of the Year. He beat out pro golfer Jordan Spieth and horse racing's Triple Crown winner American Pharoah for the award.

SET NBA RECORD FOR NUMBER OF THREE-POINT SHOTS IN A GAME

On November 7, 2016, in a home matchup against the New Orleans Pelicans, Curry scored 46 points, pulled down five rebounds, and dished out five assists to lead all scorers and the Warriors to a 116–106 victory. The victory over the Pelicans included an astounding 13 for 17 shooting from beyond the three-point line. This mark gave him the NBA record for the number of three-pointers made in an NBA game. This passed the old record of 12 made three-pointers that was set by Kobe Bryant as a member of the Los Angeles Lakers in 2003, which was tied by Donyell Marshall (with the Toronto Raptors) in 2005 and, of course, by Curry himself the previous season in a February 27, 2016, game against the Oklahoma City Thunder.

Curry, one game after setting the NBA record for consecutive games with at least one three-pointer made at 157, sets another record for most three-pointers in a game at 13.

Curry has achieved the rare feat of having a season in which he shot at least 50 percent from the field, 40 percent behind the arc, and 90 percent from the line.

TEXT-DEPENDENT QUESTIONS

1. How many three-pointers did Curry make in a November 7, 2016, game against the San Antonio Spurs to establish the NBA record for most three-pointers made in a single game?

2. What is the 50–40–90 club? How many players in the history of the league are members of the club? How many players have made the 50–40–90 club in multiple seasons?

3. How many MVP awards has Curry won in his NBA career? How many NBA Championships has he won as a member of the Golden State Warriors?

RESEARCH PROJECT

The 50–40–90 club is a unique honor in that it truly recognizes shooting and scoring excellence in the league. Having to achieve consistency across all shooting disciplines is a reason why only eight players have done so in the regular season. As difficult as it is to achieve 50–40–90 in the regular season, could you imagine a player doing so in the playoffs? Well, it has happened once and almost for a second time. Find the player who accomplished the mark in the playoffs (name, team, year) and the other player who narrowly missed joining the 50–40–90 playoff club.

WORDS TO UNDERSTAND

commensurate: Similar to or the same as

hone: To make more acute or effective; improve; perfect

pedigree: An ancestral line; line of descent; lineage; ancestry

province: A legislative district or region in a country

CHAPTER 2

THE ROAD TO THE TOP

STEPHEN CURRY'S PERFORMANCE AS A PLAYER

Wardell Stephen Curry II was born on March 14, 1988, in Akron, Ohio. His parents Sonya and Dell Curry raised him in Charlotte, North Carolina, for the first 10 years of his life while Dell played guard for the Charlotte Hornets. From the ages of 11 to 13, Curry lived in Toronto, Ontario, Canada, as his father finished his career with the Toronto Raptors. He returned to Charlotte for the end of the 2001–2002 season at the end of Dell's NBA playing career, and in autumn 2003, enrolled in Charlotte Christian School (nickname: "Knights") for high school.

While living in Canada, Curry played basketball in the eighth grade for Queensway Christian College and was a member of a local club basketball team (Toronto 5–0) that traveled across the **province** of Ontario. The team he played on won a provincial championship in 2002, posting a 33–4 record. Curry's talent as a shooter began to emerge during that time, which was even more remarkable considering that, according to former teammates and friends, he was often the smallest kid on the team.

After little interest from major programs, Curry chose to play near home at Davidson College, where he had a storied career.

Curry's skills from outside the three-point line were **honed** throughout high school and into college, where he played for Davidson College in Davidson, North Carolina (nickname: Wildcats). Davidson College is also where the 28th president of the United States, Woodrow Wilson, attended school briefly in 1873–1874. By the time Curry entered the NBA, he had developed into a feared shooter and was destined for greatness.

Curry was a member of the All-Rookie Team in 2010. He has been named Player of the Month on 10 occasions in his career and Player of the Week 13 times. Curry has been described as one of—if not the greatest—shooter in the history of the NBA. That is quite a compliment when you consider players like Reggie Miller (Indiana Pacers), Paul Westphal (Phoenix Suns), and "Pistol" Pete Maravich (New Orleans Jazz) were all considered the greatest shooters in their careers. Only time will tell where Curry will rank, but it certainly seems that he has set himself in a class by himself when it comes to shooting excellence.

Stephen's father Dell had a long NBA career, playing most of his seasons with Charlotte, where Stephen eventually went to high school.

NBA DRAFT DAY 2009 SIGNIFICANT ACCOUNTS

- Stephen Curry was selected by Golden State with the seventh pick in the first round of the 2009 NBA draft.

- The 2009 NBA draft was held at Madison Square Garden located in New York, New York, on June 25, 2009.

- Curry was the fifth guard drafted in the 2009 NBA draft.

- After the selection of Hasheem Thabeet by the Memphis Grizzlies with the second pick, Curry was one of five guards selected in a row with picks three through seven in the first round.

- He was one of 17 guards selected in round 1 of the draft

and 30 guards drafted overall in both rounds 1 and 2 (out of 60 players drafted). Twenty-seven forwards and only three centers were drafted in 2009.

- Curry was one of three sons of former NBA players taken in the first 15 picks of the 2009 draft. The others were Gerald Henderson's son Gerald Jr. (number 12 to Charlotte) and Darren Daye's son Austin (number 15 to Detroit).

- The Minnesota Timberwolves had the most draft selections in 2009 with six. Ten teams had one pick each in the draft: Boston Celtics, Denver Nuggets, Golden State Warriors, Los Angeles Clippers, New Jersey Nets, New Orleans Hornets, New York Knicks, Philadelphia 76ers, Toronto Raptors, and Washington Wizards.

- The University of North Carolina (nickname: Tar Heels) placed the most players in the 2009 draft with four: Tyler Hansbrough (number 13, by the Indiana Pacers); Ty Lawson (number 18, by the Minnesota Timberwolves); Wayne Ellington (number 28, also by Minnesota); and Danny Green (number 46, by the Cleveland Cavaliers).

Source: https://stats.nba.com/draft/history/?Season=2009 – NBA draft information for 2009 NBA Draft.

HIGH SCHOOL

After Curry's father, Dell, completed his NBA career with the Toronto Raptors in 2002, Stephen and his family left Canada and moved back to Charlotte, North Carolina, where he attended high school. During the three years Curry played at Charlotte Christian School, he led his Knights squad to three North Carolina state boys' basketball championships. He also earned all-conference and all-state honors during his time in high school.

Curry's play was good enough to earn him three stars as a potential recruit by both *Scout* and *Rivals* magazines. His height of six feet two inches (1.88 m) and weight of 163 pounds (74 kg) made him an undersized prospect, however, and the most he received in offers was a walk-on spot at Virginia Tech University (where his father Dell was a star). He instead signed a letter of intent in September 2005 to attend Davidson College, a school that had recruited him since his sophomore year in high school.

BATTLE OF FUTURE NBA STARS

During Curry's senior year in high school at Charlotte Christian School, he had the opportunity to match his talents with those of another up-and-coming talent, Jodie Meeks. Meeks, who recently played with the Milwaukee Bucks, led Norcross (GA) High School to a state championship in 2006. He had the opportunity to face Curry's Knights in a 2005 matchup. The Curry-led Knights beat the Meeks-led Blue Devils 64–60 in a thrilling preview of things to come for these two potential NBA stars.

Curry and Jodie Meeks battle in a prep game, displaying the skills that would take them eventually to the hardwood courts of the NBA.

COLLEGE

Curry's impact on the Wildcats of Davidson was felt the moment he stepped on campus. In his first year at Davidson, he was second in the nation for freshman scoring (behind Kevin Durant of the University of Texas). He led the Wildcats to a 29–5 record and the Southern Conference title. He also set the NCAA freshman record for three-point shots made.

The Wildcats finish in 2007 was good enough for them to receive a bid to the NCAA Men's Basketball Tournament as a 13 seed. Curry put up a 30-point effort against the University of Maryland, which won the game, 84–70. Curry's sophomore year saw him attain his present height of six feet three inches (1.91 m) and lead the Southern Conference with 25.9 points per game. The Wildcats

Curry played three years at Davidson, where the Wildcats played their home games at John M. Belk Arena.

won the conference title for a second year with a 26–6 record, including a perfect 20–0 in the conference. He rose to the attention of NBA scouts by becoming the fourth player in college basketball history to average 30 points or more a game in his first four NCAA tournament games.

Davidson had an impressive run in the 2008 tournament with victories over seventh-seeded Gonzaga University Bulldogs, second-seeded Georgetown University Hoyas, and then the fourth-seeded University of Wisconsin Badgers in the tournament's Sweet 16 to advance to the Elite 8 (quarterfinals). There Davidson lost a close 59–57 game to eventual champion University of Kansas Jayhawks. Curry finished his college career in his junior year, averaging 28.6 points a game and dropping 26 points on Saint Mary's College (nickname: "Gaels") in a second-round loss in the National Invitational Tournament (NIT).

These are Curry's statistics for the three seasons that he played at Davidson:

Season	G	FG	FGA	3P	FT	TRB	AST	STL	BLK	PTS	PTS	TRB	AST
2006–07	34	242	523	122	124	157	95	62	6	730	21.5	4.6	2.8
2007–08	36	317	656	162	135	165	104	73	14	931	25.9	4.6	2.9
2008–09	34	312	687	130	220	151	189	86	8	974	28.6	4.4	5.6
TOTALS	**104**	**871**	**1,866**	**414**	**479**	**473**	**388**	**221**	**28**	**2,635**	**25.3**	**4.5**	**3.7**

Curry left Davidson after his junior year and entered the 2009 NBA draft. He was named a first-team All-American and left college as the NCAA scoring leader for the 2008–2009 season.

Curry left the pristine grounds of Davidson behind in 2009, skipping his senior season for the bright lights of the NBA draft.

NBA

Five players drafted in 2009 have scored 10,000 or more points in their NBA careers: James Harden (18,627 points), Stephen Curry (16,315 points), DeMar DeRozan (14,931points), Blake Griffin (13,200 points) , and Jrue Holiday (10,148 points). Blake Griffin, the number-one draft selection in 2009 (from the University of Oklahoma) broke his kneecap in preseason and did not play in the 2009–2010 season; he was named the NBA Rookie of the Year in the

Curry's first 10 years in the NBA have him on track for the Basketball Hall of Fame.

2010 season. Tyreke Evans, the fourth overall draft selection in 2009 (from the University of Memphis), was named NBA Rookie of the Year.

Through his first nine NBA seasons, Curry kept pace with some of the greatest NBA players, both past and present. His numbers, in terms of total scoring, three-pointers, free throws, rebounds, steals, and points scored are **commensurate** with those of Dwyane Wade, Jerry West, James Harden, and Kobe Bryant, among others.

Here's how Curry's numbers (through the end of the 2017–2018 NBA season) look as compared to those of other great shooters through their first nine NBA seasons.

Players with career totals similar to Curry after nine seasons:

Season	TEAM	G	FG	3P	FT	TRB	AST	STL	BLK	PTS	PPG
Jerry West*	Los Angeles Lakers	612	5933	-	4,969	3,976	3,469	-	-	16,835	27.5
Dwyane Wade	Miami Heat	596	5,292	324	4,082	3,020	3,697	1,055	611	14,990	25.2
Stephen Curry†	**Golden State Warriors**	**625**	**5,017**	**2,129**	**2,271**	**2,763**	**4,227**	**1,108**	**154**	**129**	**23.1**
James Harden†	OKC Thunder, Houston Rockets	687	4,656	1,647	4,850	3,482	4,157	1,031	325	15,809	23.0
Russell Westbrook†	Oklahoma City Thunder	668	5,239	706	3,972	4,149	5,293	1,153	197	15,156	22.7
Clyde Drexler*	Portland Trailblazers	709	5,761	275	3,060	4,351	4,114	1,528	501	14,857	21.0
Kobe Bryant	Los Angeles Lakers	627	4,890	619	3,635	3,209	2,788	912	401	12,396	19.8
Walt Frazier*	New York Knicks	683	5,204	-	2,886	4,305	4,388	457	38	13,294	19.5
Chris Paul†	New Orleans Hornets, Los Angeles Clippers	617	4,036	612	2,812	2,694	6,112	1,485	54	11,496	18.6
Sidney Moncrief	Milwaukee Bucks	633	3,739	64	3,300	3,275	2,501	809	206	10,842	17.1
John Stockton*	Utah Jazz	734	3,425	311	2,473	1,870	8,352	1,832	142	9,634	13.1

* - Basketball Hall of Fame member

† - active

THE FAMILY CURRY

Unlike his NBA superstar brother, Seth Curry has struggled to make a mark in the NBA, playing with six organizations in five seasons since going undrafted after college.

Stephen Curry comes with a basketball **pedigree**. His father, Dell, played in the league for 16 seasons with various clubs while his brother, Seth, is a member of the Portland Trail Blazers. Steph's Warriors swept Seth's Blazers in the 2019 Western Conference Finals playoff matchup. The Curry trio all play the guard position and have done well, respectively, in their NBA careers. Here is how their numbers stack up to one another:

Player	G	FG	FG%	3P	3P%	FT	FT%	TRB	AST	STL	PPG
Stephen Curry	694	5,649	47.7%	2,483	43.6%	2,534	90.5%	3,132	4,588	1,200	23.5
Dell Curry	1,083	5,090	45.7%	1,245	40.2%	1,245	84.3%	2,617	1,909	985	11.7
Seth Curry	192	653	46.7%	686	43.9%	174	84.5%	362	323	139	9.3

From high school to college to the NBA , Curry continued to develop and grow into a top performer. His improvement over the years set the stage for what would be his eventual place among the best players in the league.

TEXT-DEPENDENT QUESTIONS

1. How many seasons did Curry's father Dell play in the NBA?

2. How many points per game did Curry average in his sophomore year at Davidson College? How many points per game did he average in his junior year at Davidson?

3. What current NBA player (and teammate) did he finish behind in his freshman year for the NCAA freshman scoring title?

RESEARCH PROJECT

Fathers and sons form a long tradition of having played in the NBA almost since the time of the league's formation in 1949. It is interesting to note how many of these pairings (or trios as in the case of Dell, Stephen, and Seth Curry) have occurred. Looking back through the nearly 70-year history of the NBA, how many father-son(s) combinations can you find? As an added bonus, are there any combinations of fathers who have played in the NBA and daughters who have played in the WNBA that you can find? (The answer is, "yes!") Finally, to make things more interesting, are there any combinations of mothers who have played in the WNBA and sons who played in the NBA? (There is at least one, but the answer should be two!)

 WORDS TO UNDERSTAND

elite: Superior in quality, rank, skill, etc.

ligaments: Tough, fibrous bands of tissue connecting the articular extremities of bones or supporting an organ in place

precursor: Something that comes before something else and that often leads to or influences its development

CHAPTER 3

ON THE COURT

CURRY'S NBA ACCOMPLISHMENTS

Curry began play in the NBA for the Golden State Warriors in the 2009–2010 season. He has, in 10 full seasons, accomplished quite a bit as a player. He is a multiple Most-Valuable-Player recipient. Curry has been to six NBA all-star games. He has moved to number one all-time for three-pointers made in the playoffs in league history, and is the only player with more than 400. He has been called one of the greatest shooters in the game, which puts him in a very elite group.

What else has Curry accomplished in his NBA career? Here are a few select highlights of his NBA career accomplishments.

In 2015, Curry made 805 baskets to lead the league.

- Led the league in field goals during the 2015–2016 season with 805.

- Led the league five consecutive seasons (2012–2017) in made three-pointers. He also led the league over that same five-year period in three-pointers attempted.

- His 2,483 made three-pointers for his NBA career puts him at number three on the all-time list.

- He led the league in steals in each of the two years he won his MVP awards (2015: 163 steals; 2016: 169 steals).

- He shot more than 90 percent from the free throw line five times in his career (2011, 2015, 2016, 2018 and 2019).

- He is ranked in the top 25 on the career points-per-game list, averaging for his career 23.5. He led the league in 2016 with a 30.1 points-per-game average.

STEPHEN CURRY

POINT GUARD

- Date of birth: March 14, 1988

- Height: six feet three inches (1.91 m) Weight: Approximately 190 pounds (86 kg)

- College: Davidson College (nickname: "Wildcats")

- Drafted in the first round in 2009 (seventh pick, overall) by the Golden State Warriors

- Two-time NBA Most Valuable Player (2015, 2016)

- Three-time NBA champion (2015, 2017, 2018)

- NBA scoring champion and steals leader for 2016

- Six-time NBA All-Star (2014–2019)

- Three-time All-NBA first team (2015, 2016, 2019)

- Member of the 50–40–90 club, which recognizes players who in the same season have made at least 50 percent of their field goals, 40 percent of their three-point shots, and 90 percent of their free throws

GOLDEN STATE
WARRIORS

CURRY ON THE HARDWOOD

The numbers that Curry has put up year after year since coming into the NBA have been outstanding. Since a shortened 2011–2012 season when he had torn **ligaments** in his ankle repaired, he has averaged 20 points or more a game in each of the subsequent seasons (2012–2018). His average during the 2015–2016 season, 30.1, topped all scorers in the NBA and was one of the reasons why he was selected as the league's MVP for the second year in a row.

Curry likes to put his hands on the ball whenever he has the opportunity, both on the offensive and defensive ends. He has led the league in ball thefts on two separate occasions, and his career steals total already places him in the top 100 on the NBA all-time career list. His more than 4,500 assists ranks him in the top 80 on the career list.

One of the NBA's best free throw shooters, Curry has led the league in free throw percentage four times, with a better than 90 percent career average.

Here are his year-to-year statistics through 2019:

CAREER STATISTICS

Season	G	FG	3P	FT	TRB	AST	STL	BLK	PTS	PPG
2009–10	80	528	166	177	356	472	152	19	1399	17.5
2010–11	74	505	151	212	286	432	109	20	1373	18.6
2011–12	26	145	55	38	88	138	39	8	383	14.7
2012–13	78	626	272	262	314	539	126	12	1786	22.9
2013–14	78	652	261	308	334	666	128	14	1873	24.0
2014–15	80	653	286	308	341	619	163	16	1900	23.8
2015–16	79	805	402	363	430	527	169	15	2375	30.1
2016–17	79	675	324	325	353	524	142	17	1999	25.3
2017–18	51	428	212	278	261	310	80	8	1346	26.4
2018–19	69	632	354	263	369	361	92	25	1,881	27.3
TOTAL	**694**	**5,649**	**2,483**	**2,534**	**3,132**	**4,588**	**1,200**	**154**	**16,315**	**23.5**

Highlighted areas indicate statistics where he ranked first for the season in that category.

Additionally, Curry has made playoff appearances in seven consecutive seasons, beginning in 2013. He has appeared in 112 playoff games in his career through 2019, acquiring three NBA championships, including the Warriors' first championship in 40 years in 2015.

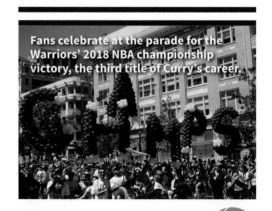

Fans celebrate at the parade for the Warriors' 2018 NBA championship victory, the third title of Curry's career.

PLAYOFF STATISTICS

Season	G	FG	3P	FT	TRB	AST	STL	BLK	PTS	PPG
2012–13	12	102	42	35	46	97	20	2	281	23.4
2013–14	7	51	22	37	25	59	12	1	161	23.0
*2014–15**	*21*	*200*	*98*	*96*	*105*	*134*	*39*	*3*	*594*	*28.3*
2015–16	18	148	80	76	99	93	26	5	452	25.1
*2016–17**	*17*	*151*	*72*	*103*	*106*	*114*	*34*	*4*	*477*	*28.1*
*2017–18**	*15*	*137*	*64*	*45*	*91*	*81*	*26*	*11*	*383*	*25.5*
2018–19	*22*	*190*	*92*	*148*	*132*	*126*	*24*	*4*	*620*	*28.2*
TOTAL	**112**	**979**	**470**	**540**	**604**	**704**	**181**	**30**	**2,968**	**26.5**

Won NBA Championship

Curry's 470 three-point shots made rank him first overall in NBA history. His 1,171 three-point attempts in the playoffs rank him first all-time as well. Curry's 26.5 points per playoff game rank him eighth on the career list, 2.6 points per game behind teammate Kevin Durant (whose 29.1 ppg rank him fourth all-time).

Curry played in every All-Star game from 2014 to 2018, including the 2016 event in Toronto.

Curry appeared in six consecutive All-Star games from 2014 to 2019. He averaged 17 points a game in these six appearances and has accomplished the following stats:

ALL-STAR GAME STATISTICS

Season	G	FG	3P	FT	TRB	AST	STL	BLK	PTS	PPG
2013–14	1	4	2	2	3	11	1	0	12	12.0
2014–15	1	6	3	0	9	5	1	0	15	15.0
2015–16	1	10	6	0	5	6	4	0	26	26.0
2016–17	1	8	5	0	4	6	1	0	21	21.0
2017–18	1	4	3	0	6	5	1	0	11	11.0
2018-19	1	6	4	1	9	7	0	0	17	17.0
TOTAL	**6**	**38**	**23**	**3**	**36**	**40**	**8**	**0**	**102**	**17.0**

Finally, and appropriately, Curry is the career NBA Finals leader in three-pointers made at 121, 35 more than the career finals runner-up, LeBron James (86). His 43 Finals steals place him in the top twenty all-time and 741 points rank him 14th on the career list.

 # INJURY CANNOT SIDELINE CURRY'S CAREER

Curry has suffered a series of ankle injuries throughout his career. Having ankle issues is not something that is good for a premier shooter like Curry. After an injury-shortened 2011–2012 season (in which he appeared in only 26 games), he overcame the injury and stayed healthy for the next three seasons, helping the Warriors reach the NBA Finals for the first time in 40 years. The injury bug rose again and has affected Curry in each season since 2015, but it has not stopped him from giving his all for his team. Unfortunately, the Warriors are only as good as Curry's ankle.

Curry suffered an ankle injury during a December 8, 2010, game at San Antonio, which the Warriors lost 111–94. Although he ended up playing 74 games during the 2010–2011 season, he required surgery that kept him sidelined for most of the next season.

The Warriors franchise began in Philadelphia and was the team that originally drafted the legendary Wilt Chamberlain (#13).

The Golden State Warriors have existed since 1946. The original Warriors franchise made its home in the City of Brotherly Love, Philadelphia. The team was a founding member of the Basketball Association of America (BAA), an early **precursor** to the National Basketball Association (which was a merger of the BAA and former National Basketball League—NBL—that came together in 1949) along with the Baltimore Bullets (now Washington Wizards) and Minneapolis Lakers (now Los Angeles Lakers).

NBA legend Rick Barry led the Warriors to the NBA title in 1975.

The Warriors won the first BAA championship in 1947. After the merger of the BAA and NBL to form the NBA, the Philadelphia Warriors became champions again in 1956. Although the team failed to win a championship led by the great Wilt Chamberlain, in 1962, the franchise moved from Philadelphia to San Francisco. In 1971, the team took on an area name, Golden State, to represent the cities of San Francisco and Oakland, and currently play in

Oakland. Rick Barry led the 1974–1975 squad that won the franchise's third championship. Even with players such as Hall-of-Fame forward Chris Mullin and Tim Hardaway leading the team, it wasn't until Curry (in 2015) and the addition of Kevin Durant (2017, 2018) that the Warriors would add three more championships for a total of six.

Here is a list of the top five players in Philadelphia/San Francisco/Golden State Warrior history (including Stephen Curry) compared over the first five seasons they played for the franchise:

Season	TEAM	Years	G	FG	FT	TRB	AST	STL	BLK	PTS	PPG
Wilt Chamberlain*	Philadelphia/ San Francisco Warriors	1959–65	429	7,216	3,351	10,768	1,303	-	-	17,783	41.5
Rick Barry*†	San Francisco/ Golden State Warriors	1965–67 1972–75	358	3,804	2,328	3,078	1,387	173	40	9,936	27.8
Chris Mullin*	Golden State Warriors	1985–90	317	2,432	1,422	1,218	1,224	518	153	6,413	20.2
Tim Hardaway‡	Golden State Warriors	1989–93 1994–95	346	2,709	1,235	1,316	3,316	708	57	7,090	20.5
Stephen Curry	Golden State Warriors	2009–14	374	2,769	1,139	1,564	2,551	636	80	7,698	20.6

*NBA Hall-of-Fame Inductee.
†Barry played in the American Basketball Association (ABA) from 1967–1972 before returning to the Warriors for the 1972–1973 season.
‡Hardaway missed the 1993–1994 season due to injury.

Only Rick Barry and Curry won championships as members of the Warriors. Barry was a champion in 1975 while Curry holds three championship rings from the 2015, 2017, and 2018 NBA Finals.

TEXT-DEPENDENT QUESTIONS

1. What year did Curry win his second league Most Valuable Player award? What was his points-per-game average for that season?

2. What years did he win an NBA Championship as a member of the Golden State Warriors?

3. How many seasons did he lead the league in steals? Where does Curry rank on the NBA's career steals list?

 RESEARCH PROJECT

The NBA is the result of a merger that took place between the Basketball Association of America (BAA) and National Basketball League (NBL) in August of 1949. The Warriors, originally located in Philadelphia, was one of initial teams in the league, which was formed in 1946. The Baltimore Bullets joined the league in the following year after leaving the American Basketball League (ABL). The Warriors, along with the Bullets, who have since relocated to Washington, DC, to become the Wizards, are still in existence.

It is interesting to see how sports leagues evolve and how competing leagues come together to form those that we are familiar with today. Research all of the NBA franchise histories, and detail in a chart where the franchise originated, what year it was founded, what year it moved, and any name changes that occurred.

WORDS TO UNDERSTAND

clutch: Successful in a crucial situation

dividend: An advantage or benefit that you get because of something you have done

precocious: Exhibiting mature qualities at an unusually early age

CHAPTER 4

WORDS COUNT

When the time comes to address the media before or after a game, players either retreat to the comfort of traditional phrases that avoid controversy (Cliché City) or they speak their mind with refreshing candor (Quote Machine).

Here are 10 quotes from Stephen Curry, compiled in part from the website AZQuotes.com, with some insight as to the context of what he is talking about or referencing:

> "I've never been afraid of big moments. I get butterflies. I get nervous and anxious, but I think those are all good signs that I'm ready for the moment."

Curry is by no means one of the biggest players, but his play speaks to more than his size. It may seem that when he steps back and effortlessly launches a three-pointer or "d's up" on an offensive player and takes the ball away, he's confident and always in control. This quote exposes the truth about how Curry approaches the game. He does not fear big games or the chance to make a **clutch** free throw or layup to win the game. That does not mean, however, that he is not nervous in anticipation of what he needs to do as a shooter and a leader to help his team win. Being nervous must work because the Warriors have ridden Curry to three championships and a 70-win season in his career.
Rating: Quote Machine

"**Doesn't matter where you come from, what you have or don't have... all you need to have is ... an undying passion for what you do and what you choose to do in this life, and a relentless drive and the will to do whatever it takes to be successful in whatever you put your mind to.**"

Only one school pursued Curry when he was looking to play basketball at the collegiate level, but his determination while at Davidson brought him the attention and prominence he needed to take his game to the next level. He believes that his personal and professional success come from hard work and dedication to the craft that he has committed to, which has paid huge **dividends** for him so far, a sentiment we have heard many times before. **Rating: Cliché City**

Curry works hard on both the offensive and defensive ends of the floor.

"If you don't fall how are you going to know what getting up is like?"

Success for players like Curry seems like it is meant to happen all of the time with little or no effort. He knows this not the case. Curry's success in life and on the hardwood has been paid for by the many times when he was not successful. The quote is certainly not an original, but it is a good reminder that to stand you have to fall. The opposite of success is failure, and to know true success in life means that you would have had to have failed or fallen down to learn how to get back up and try again. If Curry had not been injured prior to the 2011–2012 NBA season, he may not have learned how to recover and make himself a stronger, more reliable component of the Warriors' championship teams.

Rating: Cliché City

Curry smiles on the bench during an easy win for Team USA. He is enjoying the success he is experiencing now having overcome doubt and being underestimated early in his basketball career.

RILEY CURRY'S SHOW-STEALING ACT

Precocious is certainly an appropriate word to use in describing Curry's eldest daughter Riley. She has spent her life watching her father (and uncle) play in the NBA and is no stranger to the camera or watching her dad being interviewed after an outstanding shooting performance. After winning a game on the road to the 2015 NBA championship (Game 1 of the Western Conference Finals against the Houston Rockets), a not-quite three-year-old Riley made an appearance at the post-game press conference. Not to be outdone, she took the mic from dad and introduced herself to the world as the Curry fans should get to know. Her performance has become meme-worthy and has many wondering if she will follow in the entertainment footsteps of her parents.

Dad may be a star on the hardwood, but daughter Riley is the one the media comes to see whenever she has a chance to get in front of a camera.

"Everything happens for a reason, and everything has a story, and if you take time to realize what your dream is and what you really want in life... whether it's sports, whether it's in other fields, you have to realize that there's always work to do."

The 2015–2016 Golden State Warriors went 73–9 to win their division and the Western Conference titles. The 73 wins were the most by an NBA team in the history of the league since the Michael Jordan–led Chicago Bulls went 72–10 in the 1995–1996 season. Curry won his second consecutive MVP award, and it appeared the team was destined to be crowned champions and the greatest team ever. Unfortunately, a LeBron James–led Cleveland Cavaliers team spoiled the party, winning the championship in a dramatic seventh game victory in Oakland. The loss certainly taught Curry to be humble and appreciate that anything you want to achieve in life comes by way of hard work—nothing is ever given to you, no matter how good you are. He went straight to his bag of clichés when asked to talk about it, however. **Rating: Cliché City**

Curry's Warriors won 73 games in 2015–2016, one more than Michael Jordan's Bulls ended up with 20 seasons earlier.

"Basketball isn't just a sport. It is an art, one that must be mastered to succeed."

This quote is a good insight into how Curry has become a master shooter. He treats the game as being something more than a competition or athletic event. It is also a form of art and entertainment. Curry is not only accomplished as an offensive player, he is also a very good defender, able to grab rebounds and go for steals. Mastering the different aspects of the game is what separates Stephen Curry from other players in the league. **Rating: Quote Machine**

"What I tell people is be the best version of yourself in anything that you do. You don't have to live anybody else's story."

It would have been easy for Curry to continue to live in the shadow of his father and the things that he did as a player, thus becoming another version of Dell Curry. No doubt many around the league felt that that might have been the case. The Warriors, however, invested a top-ten pick on him in the 2009 NBA draft because they saw a player who was not going to be a repeat of the Dell Curry story but the best version of the Stephen Curry story. **Rating: Quote Machine**

> ## "To excel at the highest level— or any level, really—you need to believe in yourself."

Only one college expressed interest in Curry—Davidson College—even though he wanted to follow in his father Dell's footsteps and play at Virginia Tech University. Despite the disinterest in him as a collegiate player, Curry focused on becoming a great player, which led to his being drafted in the first round by the Golden State Warriors. This quote, though wholly unoriginal, is a testament to his belief in his talent, which means he can achieve success at any level.

Rating: Cliché City

A lack of interest from major programs led to Curry attending nearby Davidson College.

For a person who was hardly recruited in high school and had to make a lot of noise at a mid-major program at Davidson to get noticed (even as the son of a former NBA player), Curry has a lot of confidence in himself and his abilities. Some may say too much; but however much he has, it works for him. There are few players in the NBA who would not like to trade their place with him and experience a little bit of the success that he has experienced. Perhaps they just need some of his swagger.

"On the court, I'm not afraid of anything. I try to have confidence and have a belief in myself."

Rating: Quote Machine

"Success is not an accident; success is actually a choice."

This quote is who Curry is in a nutshell. He did not become one the greatest three-point shooters in NBA history by accident or because his father was a good shooter; it came because of the choices he made to be the best three-point shooter. This includes practicing hard, working on his shot, listening to his coaches (and being willing to accept coaching), and looking for opportunities to constantly improve and get better.

The results of this approach are more than evident for him, as he has been able to win recognition as the league's Most Valuable Player twice in his career and hoist the NBA Final's trophy on three separate occasions. The choice to be successful in life is no accident. **Rating: Cliché City**

"**Kids put life into perspective. I never have a bad day. Life happens and you get bad news sometime, or things don't go your way at work—for me that might mean I lose a game or not play well—but that doesn't affect my mood from day to day. I love going home and seeing the smiles on my daughters' faces being happy to see me, and that makes everything all right.**"

It is clear that Curry loves being a family person and especially loves being a father. His three children, daughters Riley (2012) and Ryan (2015), and son Cannon (2018) mean the world to him and give him a good reason to work as hard as he does on the court. No matter how bad things get for him, whether it is losing a tough game on the court or suffering a challenging injury to his ankles, he knows that at the end of the day he will go home to his loving children and all the frustrations of the day simply melt away! **Rating: Quote Machine**

Even when the shots aren't all going down for him on the court, Curry knows he always has his family waiting for him at home.

TEXT-DEPENDENT QUESTIONS

1. What is the name of Curry's eldest daughter?

2. How many children does the Curry family have?

3. How many games did Golden State win during the 2015–2016 regular season?

RESEARCH PROJECT

Being the son of a former basketball standout can be difficult for many players to deal with because of the constant comparisons to your parent and expectations that may be higher than what other players may have dealt with. Are there any players in the league with a father (or mother) who played professionally who have had a greater career than their parent? Find three examples, and compare their careers to those of their parents.

WORDS TO UNDERSTAND

coincide: To occupy the same place in space or time

exemption: A freedom or release from some liability or requirement to which others are subject

rafters: Any of the parallel beams that support a roof

recurring: Happening or appearing multiple times

CHAPTER 5

OFF THE COURT

AT HOME WITH THE CURRY FAMILY

Curry met and married his wife Ayesha Disa Alexander in 2011. She is Canadian-American, born March 23, 1989, and raised initially in Toronto, Ontario, Canada, until age fourteen, when her family moved to Charlotte, North Carolina. She met Curry in a youth group when they were living in North Carolina. She comes from a very diverse background, her mother, Carol Alexander, being of Jamaican and Chinese descent and her father, John Alexander, of Polish and African American descent.

Ayesha worked as an actress prior to marrying Curry, appearing in several television programs. After marriage, she became a culinary chef, hosting

Curry met and married his wife Ayesha in 2011.

her own YouTube program before becoming a judge on the Food Network's *The Great American Baking Show* for several seasons. She also was the first non-celebrity to be named a spokesperson for the Covergirl brand makeup in 2017.

Ayesha and her husband reside in the San Francisco suburb of Alamo, adjacent to affluent Walnut Creek, California. The couple have three children together, including eldest child Riley (born July 19, 2012), daughter Ryan (born July 10, 2015), and their only son Canon, who was born on July 2, 2018.

BACK TO SCHOOL

While attending Davidson College, Curry wore the same number 30 that he has worn as a member of the Golden State Warriors. The things he was able to accomplish while in school, including being named to two All-American teams and leading the Wildcats to within a game of their first NCAA Final Four in school history, would certainly merit his jersey hanging high above the **rafters** at Belk Arena in Davidson, North Carolina.

Interestingly if you were to spend time at the arena watching the Wildcats play, the one thing you will not find is his number 30 jersey hanging there. That

A busy and successful career on and off the court has so far kept Curry from fulfilling his promise to get his college degree.

is because according to school policy at Davidson, no former player's uniform can be retired unless the player has graduated from the school. This policy is without any exception or **exemption**.

Curry fully understands and appreciates this policy and is not looking to be treated any different than past Wildcat players. He is quoted as saying in a 2015 ESPN online article, "I knew what I signed up for when I went to Davidson. I made a promise to coach [Bob] McKillop and my family that when I left school back in '09 that that would be accomplished—and it will be soon. Hopefully sooner than later."

It has not been through lack of effort, however, that Curry has attempted to fulfill this promise made to his coach and parents. A few obstacles have presented themselves in the years since he left Davidson, such as the demands of a professional career that **coincides** with the academic year (and the fact that the school does not offer classes during the summer), the winning of three NBA championships, representing the United States in international and Olympic competition, and raising a young family.

During the strike-shortened season of 2011–2012 (while he was recovering from a **recurring** ankle injury), Curry made an attempt at chipping away at his degree requirements and returned to Davidson. For the 2011 semester he registered for three classes, including a qualitative research course that was a requirement for his major in sociology. His celebrity lifestyle aside, he has reduced the number of credits he needs to obtain for graduation to a handful.

IN THE COMMUNITY

Curry and his wife Ayesha are involved in various charitable causes and community-based programs that support youth-healthy living and that deal with issues affecting us globally. These charities include the following:

- **Animal Rescue Foundation**—known as ARF, this Walnut Creek, California-based organization was founded by former MLB manager Tony La Russa. The purpose of ARF is to rescue dogs and cats from kill shelters and adopt them into new homes.

- **Kids Wish Network**—this organization provides hope and joy to children suffering from life-threatening illness.

- **NBA Cares**—a league program that is global in scale, addressing social issues affecting people and the communities where they live.

- **Nothing But Nets**—a campaign endorsed by the United Nations that provides protective netting to persons living in countries susceptible to the disease of malaria, which is often transmitted by mosquito bites.

Tony La Russa's Animal Rescue Foundation is one of the Currys' favorite causes.

- **Partnership for a Healthier America**—an organization that works in partnership with private businesses to address the country's growing problem with childhood obesity.

- **United Nations Foundation**—a concern of the United Nations working at promoting innovative solutions to global problems by advancing human dignity and well-being.

There are at least 11 issue areas that Curry feels passion for and supports with the money he has earned as a player. These include AIDS and HIV, animals, autism, children and youth, the environment, health, human rights and social justice, hunger relief, support of the LGBT community, peace initiatives, and issues affecting and concerning women (such as empowerment).

STEPHEN AND AYESHA CURRY FAMILY FOUNDATION

Ayesha Curry is an actress, model, and successful businesswoman who is very much involved in the charity work her husband does around the Bay area.

The Stephen and Ayesha Curry Family Foundation is the charitable foundation for the Curry family, involved in providing funding to other organizations to support their charitable areas of interest. The couple has given money to pro golfer Scott Harrington and wife Jenn, who was diagnosed with Hodgkin's lymphoma in May 2018, during a fundraiser at a Web.com PGA Tour event. They have also donated to the Sonoma County's Resilience Fund involved in relief efforts for those families impacted by the California fires of 2018 that caused widespread devastation and damage.

They have also given support to the Bushrod Community Recreation Center in North Oakland for the creation of an education lab. They have used their wealth as a way to address issues that they personally feel strongly about, providing opportunities for those with few resources or aid and comfort to others in time of need.

CELEBRITY FAMILY FEUD
AND FIRE DISASTER RELIEF

The 2018 California Wildfires, which started in February, caused widespread destruction. The fires (more than 7,900 individual fires recorded) caused nearly $3 billion in damage and killed more than 100 people, including six firefighters. The tragedy affected homes and businesses throughout the state of California. Curry—like many celebrities—responded to the needs of the community and donated money, including his $25,000 earnings from an appearance on the ABC-TV show *Celebrity Family Feud,* to the Sonoma County Resilience Fund and victims of the fires.

The Curry family (Steph, Ayesha, sister Sydel, mother Sonya, and father Dell) got together for a June 24, 2018, episode of *Celebrity Family Feud* to raise money for victims of the California wildfires.

MARKETING STEPHEN CURRY

Curry has stepped into the role of one of the NBA's newest marketing stars. His MVP awards in 2015 and 2016 put him in the same class as an endorsement star as LeBron James, teammate Kevin Durant, and former LA Laker great Kobe Bryant. Curry signed deals with brands such as Under Armour, Unilever, Degree, State Farm Insurance, and clothing retailer Express.

Curry has developed his own shoe with Under Armour called the Curry One. The shoe deal is just one of the areas that his agent, Jeff Austin of Octagon Basketball, has worked on to capitalize on the young star's growing popularity, particularly among the eighteen to thirty-four age bracket that advertisers and companies love. The relationship that Austin has with Curry is an even more special as he also represented his father, Dell, during his 16 years as a player in the NBA.

Curry is one of the league's biggest marketing stars, with a jersey that outsells LeBron James's and an impressive portfolio of endorsements.

Curry rose to number 24 on Forbes Celebrity 100 list and number eight on the list of the World's Highest-Paid Athletes for 2018. Prior to the negotiation of a contract extension with the Golden State Warriors, the only team that he has played basketball for in the NBA, he earned just over $91 million in salary. The big bumps to his pay came after his two MVP awards and the three NBA championships he helped secure for the Warriors. The extension, through the 2021–2022 season, will make him one of the highest-paid players in all of sports and adds another $166.5 million to his wallet.

SALARY

Season	Team	Salary
2009–10	Golden State Warriors	$ 2,710,560.00
2010–11	Golden State Warriors	$ 2,913,840.00
2011–12	Golden State Warriors	$ 3,117,120.00
2012–13	Golden State Warriors	$ 3,958,742.00
2013–14	Golden State Warriors	$ 9,887,642.00
2014–15	Golden State Warriors	$ 10,629,213.00
2015–16	Golden State Warriors	$ 11,370,786.00
2016–17	Golden State Warriors	$ 12,112,359.00
2017–18	Golden State Warriors	$ 34,682,550.00
		$ 91,382,812.00

CONTRACT

Season	Team	Salary
2018–19	Golden State Warriors	$ 37,457,154.00
2019–20	Golden State Warriors	$ 40,231,758.00
2020–21	Golden State Warriors	$ 43,006,362.00
2021–22	Golden State Warriors	$ 45,780,966.00
		$ 166,476,240.00

Curry and his father Dell participated in the 2016 NBA All-Star festivities in Toronto, where Dell played three seasons and Stephen sharpened his basketball skills. Those skills have earned him an All-Star status that makes him one of the highest-paid players in the NBA.

Add another $42 million a year in endorsements, and you almost feel sorry for those agencies (and schools) who passed on the smallish six feet-three inch (1.90 m) shooting guard. Curry holds no ill feelings for those who looked past him and continues to prove on the court why he is an investment worth more than his weight in gold!

TEXT-DEPENDENT QUESTIONS

1. What is the value of the contract extension Curry signed in 2018 through the 2021–2022 NBA season?

2. What is the name of Curry's charitable foundation? What are some of the key issues the foundation is involved with?

3. At what age did the Currys meet? Where did they meet?

RESEARCH PROJECT

Ayesha and Stephen Curry are a formidable couple. While his efforts have brought him to the top of his profession as a player, she has also raised her own profile and personal brand. She has taken on the role of culinary expert and is host of several food-related programs, such as Food Network's *The Great American Baking Show*. Who are some of the other NBA power couples in the league today, where both the player and his spouse are equally successful? Name the couple, the team the player is on, and some details about the activities his spouse is engaged in.

assist: a pass that directly leads to a teammate making a basket.

blocked shot: when a defensive player stops a shot at the basket by hitting the ball away.

center: a player whose main job is to score near the basket and win offensive and defensive rebounds. Centers are usually the tallest players on the court, and the best are able to move with speed and agility.

double-dribble: when a player dribbles the ball with two hands or stops dribbling and starts again. The opposing team gets the ball.

field goal: a successful shot worth two points—three points if shot from behind the three-point line.

foul: called by the officials for breaking a rule: reaching in, blocking, charging, and over the back, for example. If a player commits six fouls during the game, he fouls out and must leave play. If an offensive player is fouled while shooting, he usually gets two foul shots (one shot if the player's basket counted or three if he was fouled beyond the three-point line).

foul shot: a "free throw," an uncontested shot taken from the foul line (15 feet [4.6 m]) from the basket.

goaltending: when a defensive player touches the ball after it has reached its highest point on the way to the basket. The team on offense gets the points they would have received from the basket. Goaltending is also called on any player, on offense or defense, who slaps the backboard or touches the ball directly above the basket.

jump ball: when an official puts the ball into play by tossing it in the air. Two opposing players try to tip it to their own teammate.

man-to-man defense: when each defensive player guards a single offensive player.

officials: those who monitor the action and call fouls. In the NBA there are three for each game.

point guard: the player who handles the ball most on offense. He brings the ball up the court and tries to create scoring opportunities through passing. Good point guards are quick, good passers, and can see the court well.

power forward: a player whose main jobs are to score from close to the basket and win offensive and defensive rebounds. Good power forwards are tall and strong.

rebound: when a player gains possession of the ball after a missed shot.

roster: the players on a team. NBA teams have 12-player rosters.

shooting guard: a player whose main job is to score using jump shots and drives to the basket. Good shooting guards are usually taller than point guards but still quick.

shot clock: a 24-second clock that starts counting down when a team gets the ball. The clock restarts whenever the ball changes possession. If the offense does not shoot the ball in time, it turns the ball over to the other team.

small forward: a player whose main job is to score from inside or outside. Good small forwards are taller than point or shooting guards and have speed and agility.

steal: when a defender takes the ball from an opposing player.

technical foul: called by the official for misconduct or a procedural violation. The team that does not commit the foul gets possession of the ball and a free throw.

three-point play: a two-point field goal combined with a successful free throw. This happens when an offensive player makes a basket but is fouled in the process.

three-point shot: a field goal made from behind the three-point line.

traveling: when a player moves, taking three steps or more, without dribbling, also called "walking." The opposing team gets the ball.

turnover: when the offensive team loses the ball: passing the ball out of bounds, traveling, or double-dribbling, for example.

zone defense: when each defensive player guards within a specific area of the court. Common zones include 2-1-2, 1-3-1, or 2-3. Zone defense has only recently been allowed in the NBA.

FURTHER READING

Bevilacqua, Thomas. *Golden Age: The Brilliance of the 2018 Champion Golden State Warriors*. Chicago: Triumph Books, 2018.

Braun, Eric. *Stephen Curry*. Minneapolis, MN: Lerner Publications Company, 2017.

Emerson, John. *Stephen Curry: Rise of the Star*. Scotts Valley, CA: CreateSpace Independent Publishing Platform, 2016.

Thompson, Marcus. *Golden: The Miraculous Rise of Stephen Curry*. New York: Simon and Schuster, 2017.

Yorkey, Mike. *The Right Steph: How Stephen Curry Is Making All the Right Moves—with Humility and Grace*. Uhrichsville, OH: Barbour Publishing, Inc., 2016.

INTERNET RESOURCES

https://www.basketball-reference.com/players/c/curryst01.html
The basketball-specific resource provided by Sports Reference, LLC for current and historical statistics of Stephen Curry.

http://bleacherreport.com/nba
The official website for Bleacher Report Sport's NBA reports on each of the 30 teams.

https://www.cbssports.com/nba/teams/GS/golden-state-warriors/
The web page for the Golden State Warriors provided by CBSSports.com, providing latest news and information, player profiles, scheduling, and standings.

https://www.eastbaytimes.com/sports/golden-state-warriors/
The web page of the *East Bay Times* (Oakland) newspaper for the Golden State Warriors basketball team.

www.espn.com/nba/team/_/name/gs/golden-state-warriors
The official website of the ESPN sports network for the Golden State Warriors.

http://www.nba.com/#/
The official website of the National Basketball Association.

https://www.nba.com/warriors/
The official NBA website for the Golden State Warriors basketball team, including history, player information, statistics, and news.

https://sports.yahoo.com/nba/
The official website of Yahoo! Sports NBA coverage, providing news, statistics, and important information about the association and its 30 teams.

INDEX

INDEX

INDEX

EDUCATIONAL VIDEO LINKS

Pg. 12: http://x-qr.net/1LjN

Pg. 13: http://x-qr.net/1HwF

Pg. 14: http://x-qr.net/1JYR

Pg. 15: http://x-qr.net/1K3s

Pg. 16: http://x-qr.net/1M3M

Pg. 17: http://x-qr.net/1LRc

Pg. 18: http://x-qr.net/1KHi

Pg. 19: http://x-qr.net/1Lzw

Pg. 29: http://x-qr.net/1M03

Pg. 44: http://x-qr.net/1Ldk

Pg. 52: http://x-qr.net/1JkA

Pg. 69: http://x-qr.net/1Kip

PHOTO CREDITS

AUTHOR BIOGRAPHY

Donald Parker is an avid sports fan, author, and father. He enjoys watching and participating in many types of sports, including football, basketball, baseball, and golf. He enjoyed a brief career as a punter and defensive back at NCAA Division III Carroll College (now University) in Waukesha, Wisconsin, and spends much of his time now watching and writing about the sports he loves.